My dearest Saida
always knew that you
are more than heroic
and you can be anything

From:
Aunty Fanta
and your sister
Sheriffa

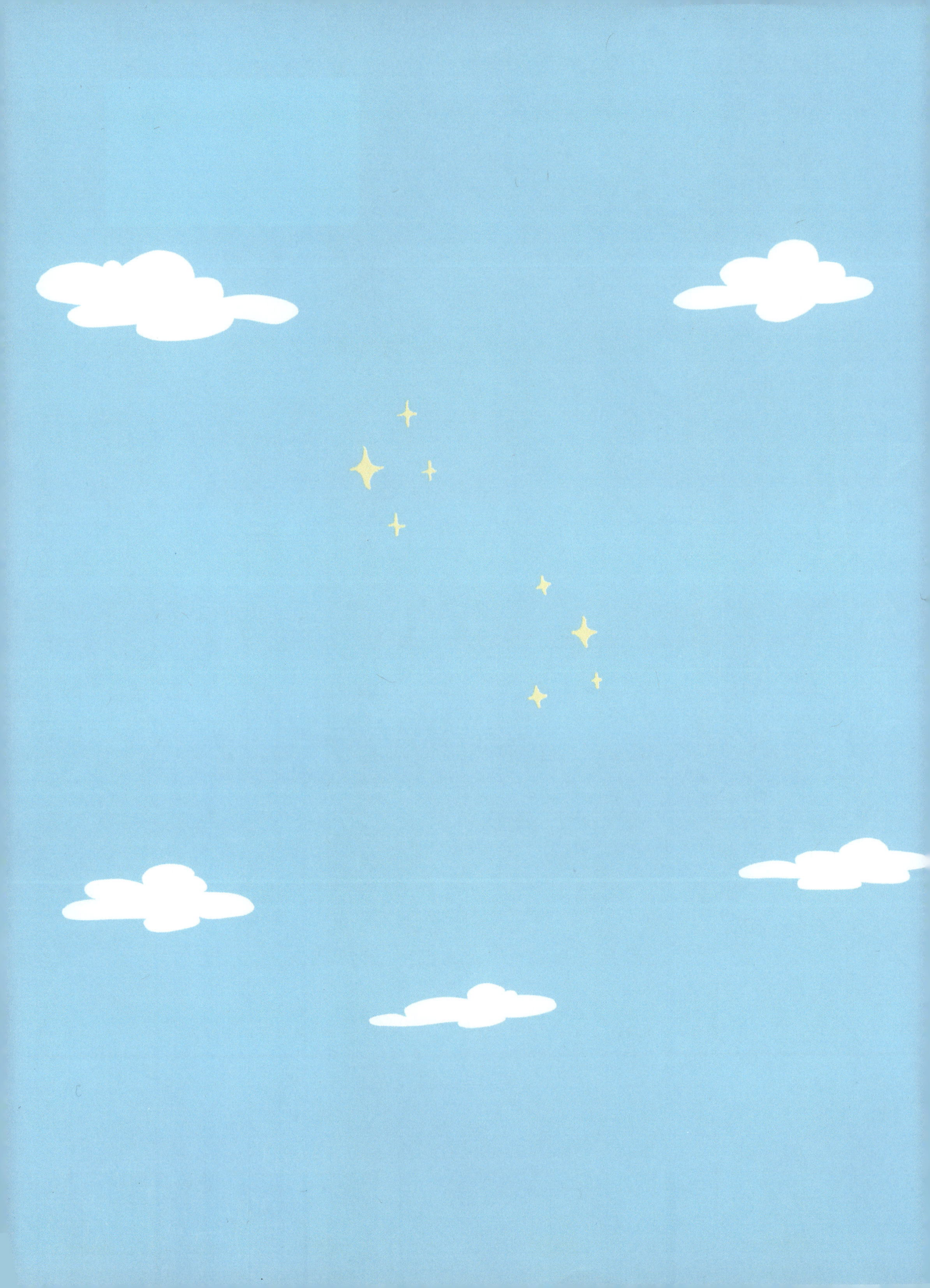

Amazing Muslim superHERoes

Layla's Healing Power

Author: Fiza Asar

Illustrator: Tehreem Iqbal

www.amazingmuslimsuperheroes.com

In the loving memory of my 'nana abba' Dr. Ikram and dedicated to all the doctors, and healers around the world who came together in a heroic way to fight against Corona. They reminded us how selflessly they do their jobs while risking their lives to save those of the others. - Fiza

Dedicated to the healthcare workers all around the world and through time who have been working hard to save lives. A special appreciation for our mothers and grandmothers who have always tended to our endless injuries and wounds during extreme play time! - Tehreem

About This Book

As Aelya's younger sister gets hurt while playing in the garden, there is panic in the house. Amidst this panic, the two sisters Zoya and Aelya, learn something amazing about nature and are mesmerised by the story of an exemplary healer from history. Layla, also known as Al-Shifa, was not just super brainy, but also extremely worried about her community's prosperity. It is no surprise, the two sisters now want to become a shero who can change the world around them into a safer and stronger place!

Boing!

From one sofa, landing on the other

Swirled in her imaginary world,

almost bumping into her brother

Whizzing by in a black cape

and bringing her speed down to zero -

Here was a seven-year old Aelya

just pretending to be her favourite superhero!

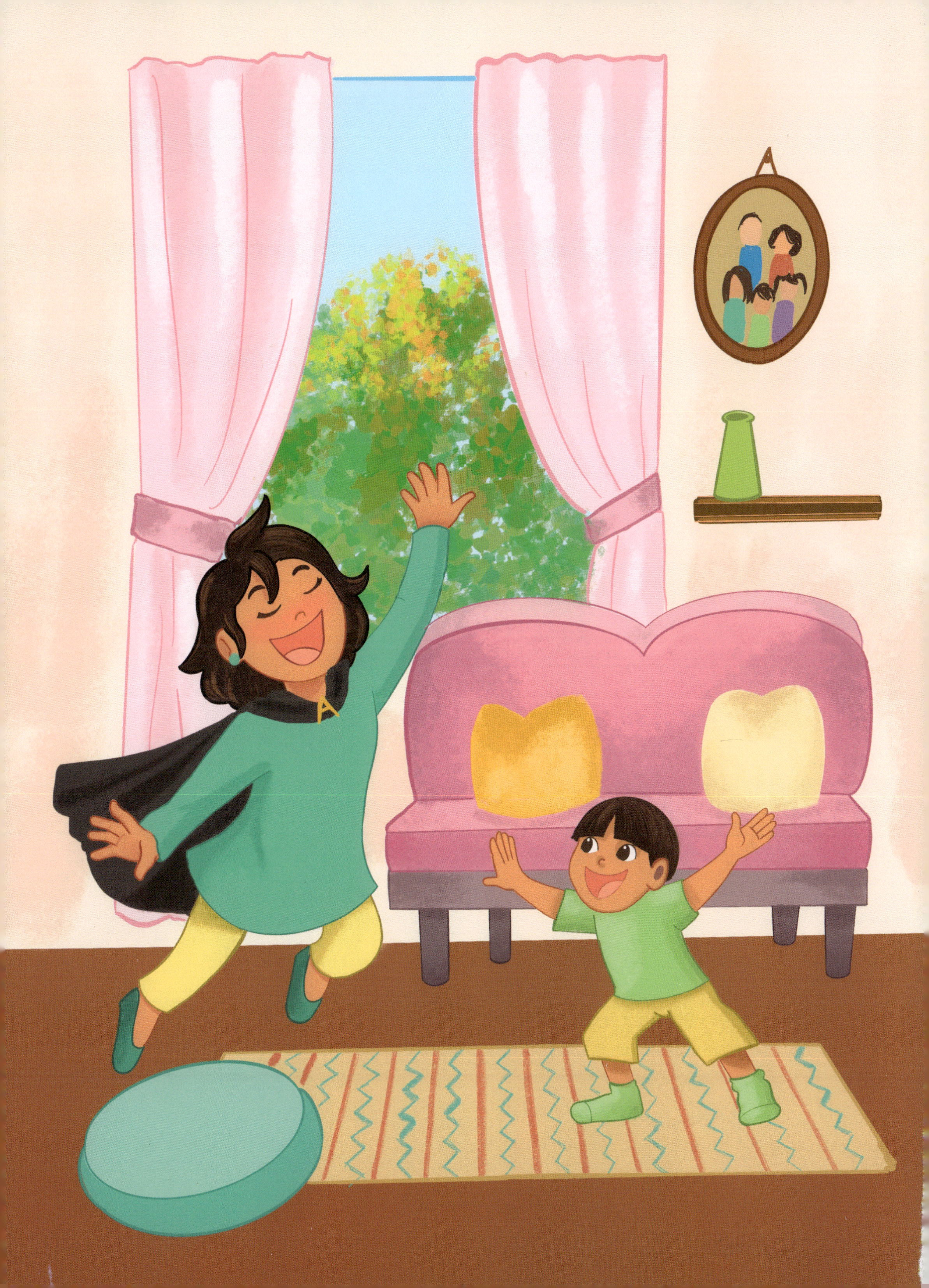

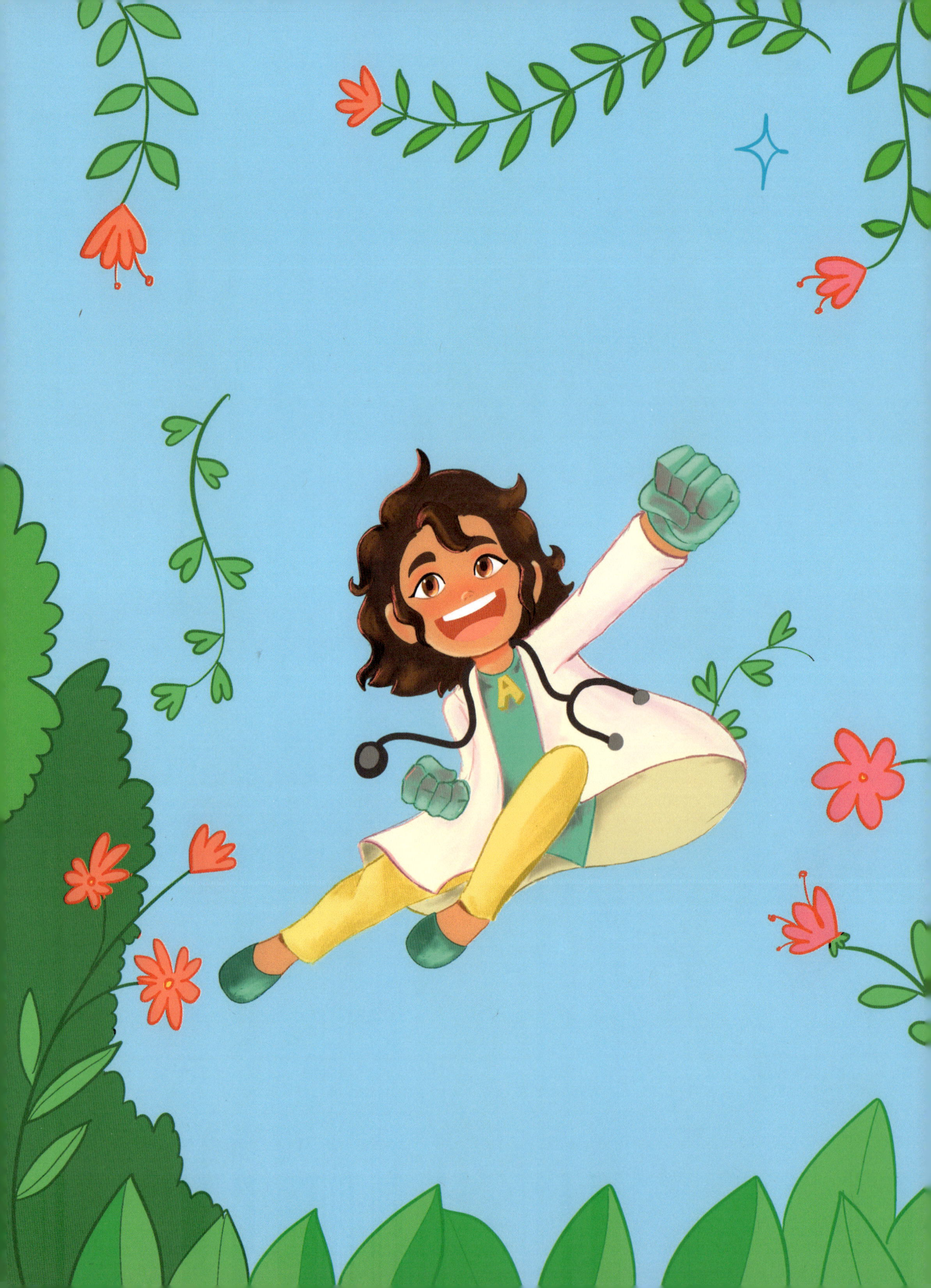

It was a beautiful Wednesday evening in Karachi. Like every Summer evening, Aelya first waited for the scorching sun to lose its blaze, and the sea breeze to cool the air before she darted out into their small garden with her sister. The two sisters put on their pretend superhero capes, grabbed their mini sets of trolls, ponies and dolls, and headed straight for the dry patch they called "The Wonder Garden."

The beautiful smell from the jasmine tree nearby wafted through the summer breeze. Their Wonder Garden was a sandy patch in the corner of the garden, under the shade of a pink bougainvillea tree, where the grass did not grow evenly. Here, their water cans made out of the measuring cups from their toy baking sets, their favourite beach bucket and the yellow spade with a purple handle lay next to the holes they had dug.

Aelya loved to plant seeds here with her sister. They collected seeds they had found in the apples, watermelons and cherries that they loved to eat. Aelya imagined magical trees and strange plants growing here between the sandy hills, where her trolls and ponies practiced their magical powers.

"Trip trap trip trap, what potion do you want from me, my little pony friend!" chanted Aelya, beaming with excitement.

"Make me turn invisible…oh wait … I'm sure I can do that myself! " said Zoya, giggling. She was holding Rainbow Dash with a twinkle in her eye.

Now Zoya, the younger sister, was this child petite
But size doesn't matter when we are speaking of bravery,
Her mind was bigger than her body,
her will was even huger you see.

So when she played out in the sand,
she seldom wore her shoes.
She didn't care about the bees and ants,
or the mud between her toes.

Zoya bent over an aloe vera plant pot that stood perched up in a corner, plucked out its stem and cracked it from between. The two sisters, eyes wide open, watched in amazement as its sticky juice oozed out.

"Here! This is the magic potion, Rainbow Dash! Drink this in the morning and you will be invisible until you eat a white button mushroom!" announced Aelya in a pretend-husky voice.

Their chitter-chatter resounded inside the house, while their mother sat with her cup of coffee, catching up on her personal projects, and their little brother played indoors with his toys.

Suddenly, Aelya called out to her mother, "Emergency! Mama! Zoya's got an ant sting!"

Mama flung her laptop to the side, and ran out to see what had happened. Zoya sat crouched on the damp grass, tears rolling down her cheeks, scratching the back of her neck frantically. The ant bite had turned into an itchy red bump and with every scratch, she was making it worse!

"Aelya, quickly grab a cube of ice from the freezer, wrap it in a tissue and bring it here please," Mama instructed Aelya while rushing to grab some Baltistani honey in a little bowl.

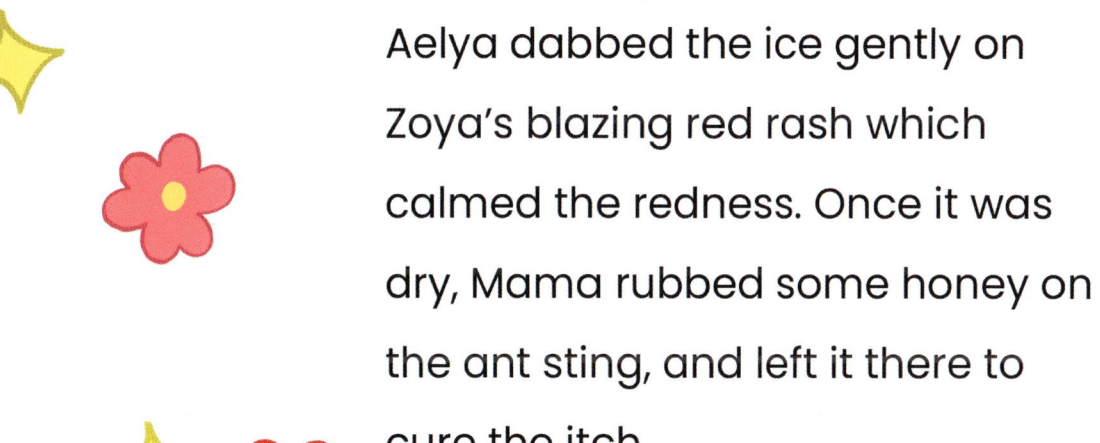

Aelya dabbed the ice gently on Zoya's blazing red rash which calmed the redness. Once it was dry, Mama rubbed some honey on the ant sting, and left it there to cure the itch.

A surely calmer Zoya, forgetting some of her fright, now instantly wanted to know, "Mama is this how Prophet Muhammad (pbuh) would cure boo-boos and ouchies? I wonder why honey though? They had pills and medicines then for sure?"

Mama smiled, "What a great question Zoya!"

In each creation of Allah
is hidden for us a gem.
You can find magical potions,
vaccines, and syrups in them!

Let me tell you today
of an awesome woman of her time
Known as Al-Shifa,
she could read and write just fine
In Mecca, when hardly twenty could write or read
Here was a lady some 1400 years ago who could heal

"Fourteen hundred! Is that like infinity??"
Zoya's mathematical mind jumped with utmost glee
"Were you a baby then mama?" she asked oh so very curiously.

SHIFA

"Oh yes, you know 1400 years ago was a time when Prophet Muhammad (pbuh) lived and preached Islam in Mecca. This was a time when a woman became one of the first Muslims to not only read and write, but also become one of the first Muslim doctors known to us. Her real name was Layla, and she was the daughter of Abdullah and Fatima, but because of her healing powers, she was known more popularly as Al-Shifa.

"Healing powers?"
"Was it like some magical power she had?"
The sisters were curious to know.

شفاء

"You see, 1400 years ago, healers searched in nature for clues. They traveled up and down plains and hills, to hotter areas and cooler patches, and collected herbs, flowers and plants that grew there. They experimented with their nectar, juices, and honey and made notes about which plants healed and which ones destroyed.

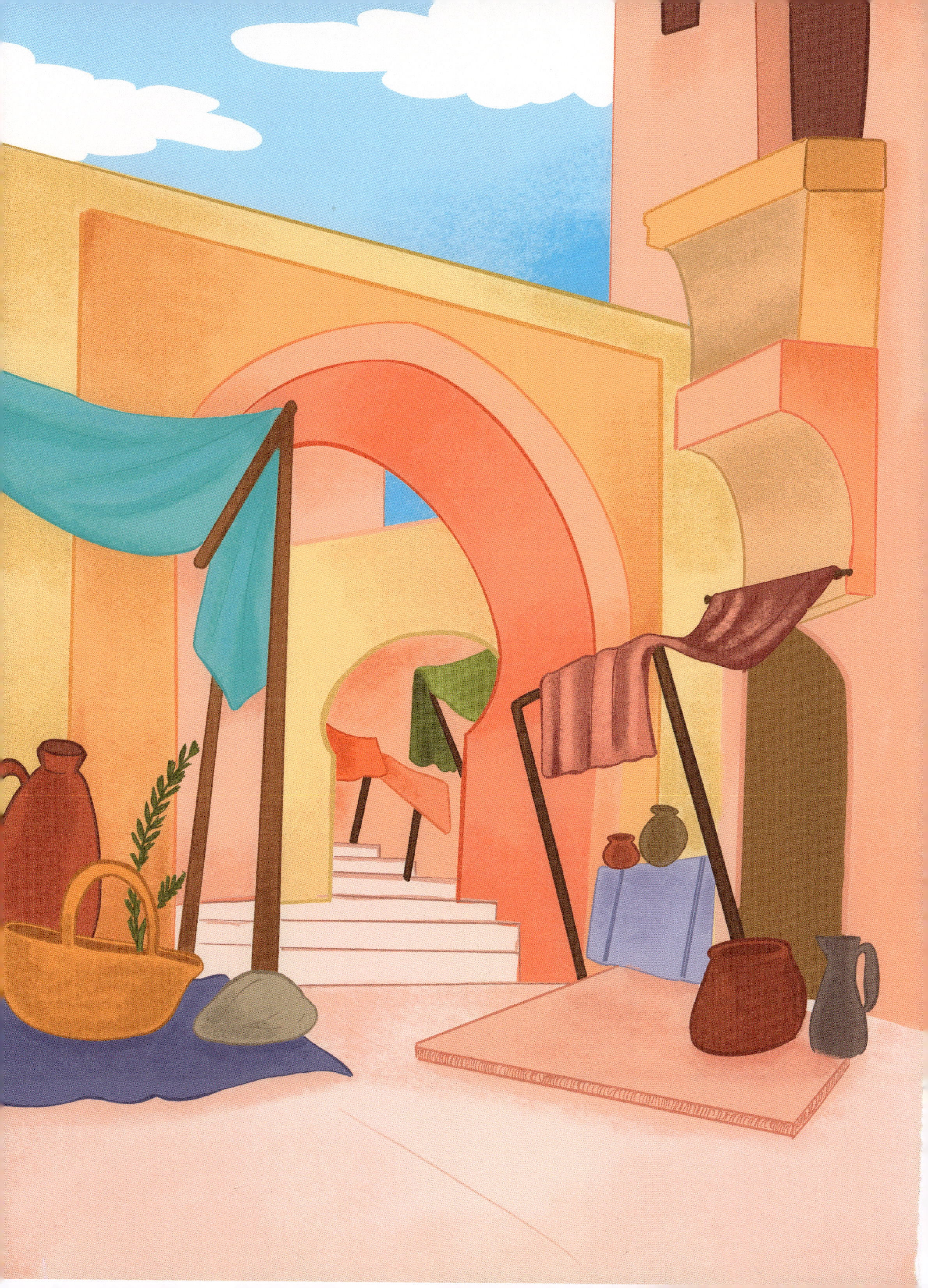

"Wow I never thought about this - Allah has made everything to help doctors!"

"And us Zoya - doctors and scientists make medicines for us!" said Aelya all-knowingly. "Wow mama, medicines have such an amazing history."

"Mama, I am imagining her like a scientist in a room
Experimenting with herbs, boiling and cooling I assume,"
Aelya jumped in, pretending to mix two potions into a fume,
Zoya began feeding the concoction to her doll in a spoon.

Smiles spread across their faces. Zoya was so mesmerized by the story of Al-Shifa, she had now forgotten all about her ouchie. Aelya, clinching on to her doll, sat enthralled, lost in her imaginary world.

"And what did she look like? What was her life like?" The two girls' thoughts were consumed.

"Well Arabia is largely a desert, where the daytime is hot and the nights are much cooler. Arabs then lived in tribes that either stayed in an area where water was close by, or were nomads which meant they moved from one place to another in search of food and livelihood.

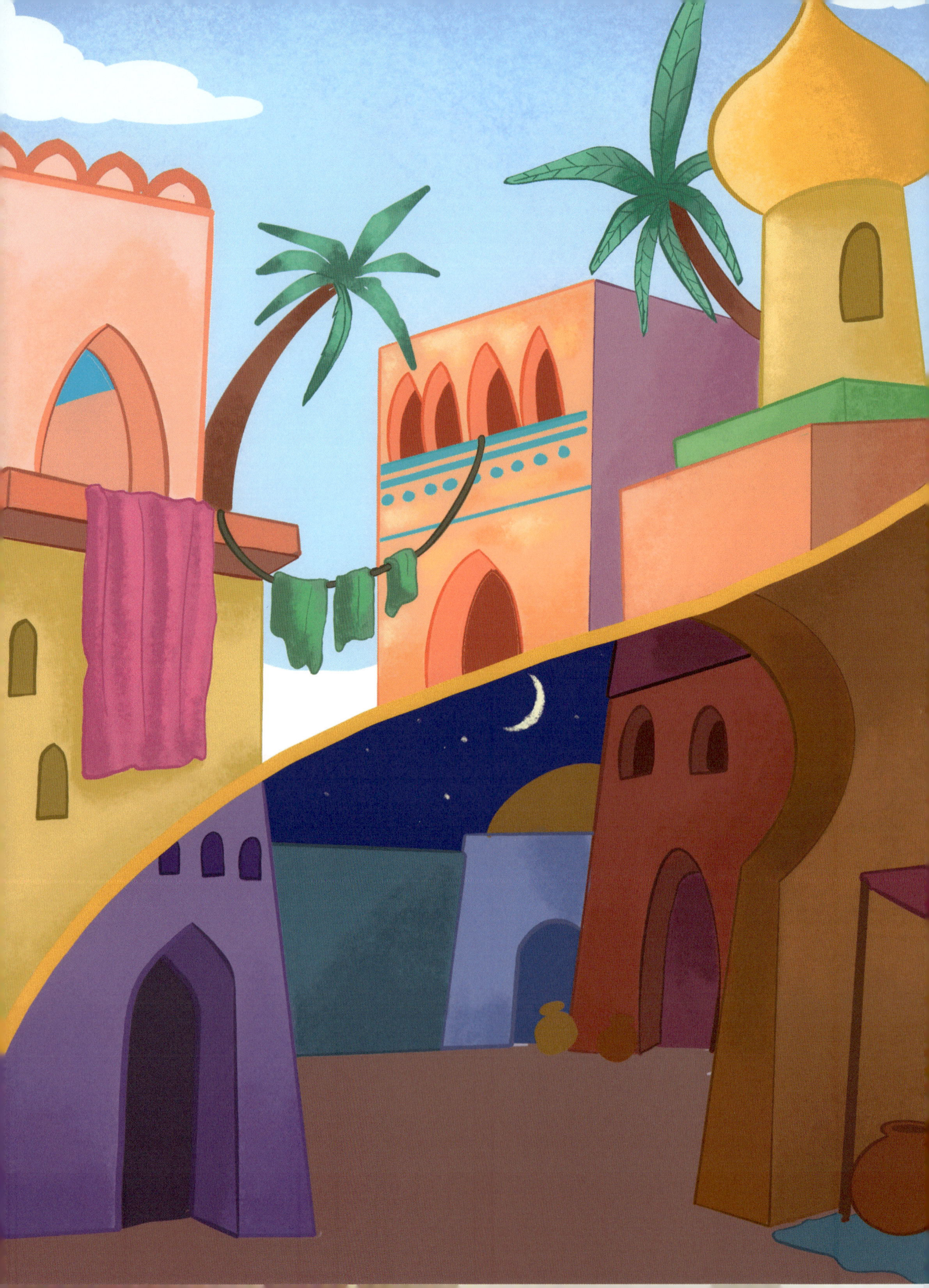

1400 years ago, their homes were not like those today. Roofs were made out of palm leaves, and walls were made out of clay. Layla's home was probably lit with an oil lamp, and I am guessing she traveled on camels, not on bicycles or cars.

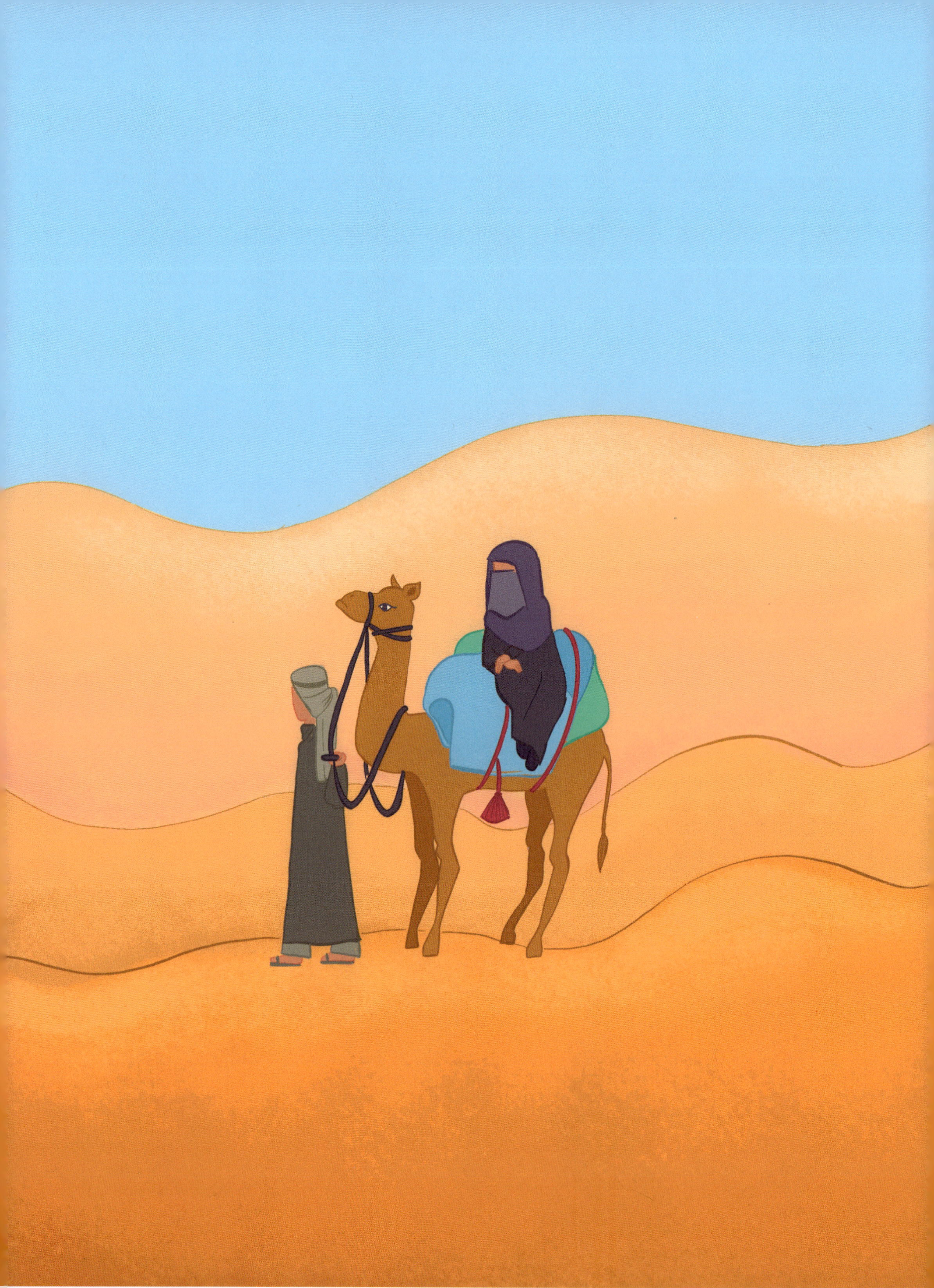

Just like you, Al-Shifa or Layla, loved the outdoors! She loved looking at plants grow, observing the bees make honey, the butterflies carrying nectars, the thorny bushes and the glossy leaves.

She was so curious that she loved experimenting to see how herbs worked and felt, and even learnt how to read and write when hardly anyone knew how to. Isn't it cool that during such times, Layla learnt to write and read and discovered the cure for ant-bite?" Mama asked, while the girls listened quietly.

"Can I tell you the most fascinating part about her?" Mama asked. The girls nodded their heads eagerly.

"Al-Shifa had two sons, and while she took care of them and her family, she also spent time teaching others what she knew. This is why she was so respected for her knowledge, that even Prophet Muhammad (PBUH) encouraged her to teach what she knew to others.

Al-Shifa' Bint 'Abdallah r.a. reported that when she was with Hafsah r.a, Prophet Muhammad (s.a.w) entered upon them and said:

أَلَا تُعَلِّمِينَ هَذِهِ رُقْيَةَ النَّمْلَةِ كَمَا عَلَّمْتِيهَا الْكِتَابَةَ؟

"Will you not teach (Hafsa r.a.) the cure for Ant bites as you have taught her writing?"

(Sunan Abi Dawud)

"So Layla aka Al-Shifa who healed everyone, was a superhero?" Aelya wanted to know.

You wonder, without super powers, what magic can you have?

When there isn't even a fancy gadget, which nasty invaders can you nab?

But you know, what makes Batman cool was his amazingly clever brain

And here was a real woman in Arabia, their very own hero, with qualities just the same

To be a doctor, you have to have something more,

Empathy and kindness - special powers you cannot ignore!

A healer's cape is the doctor's jacket, a stethoscope a magical tool

Together with brains and kindness, they fight diseases that are cruel.

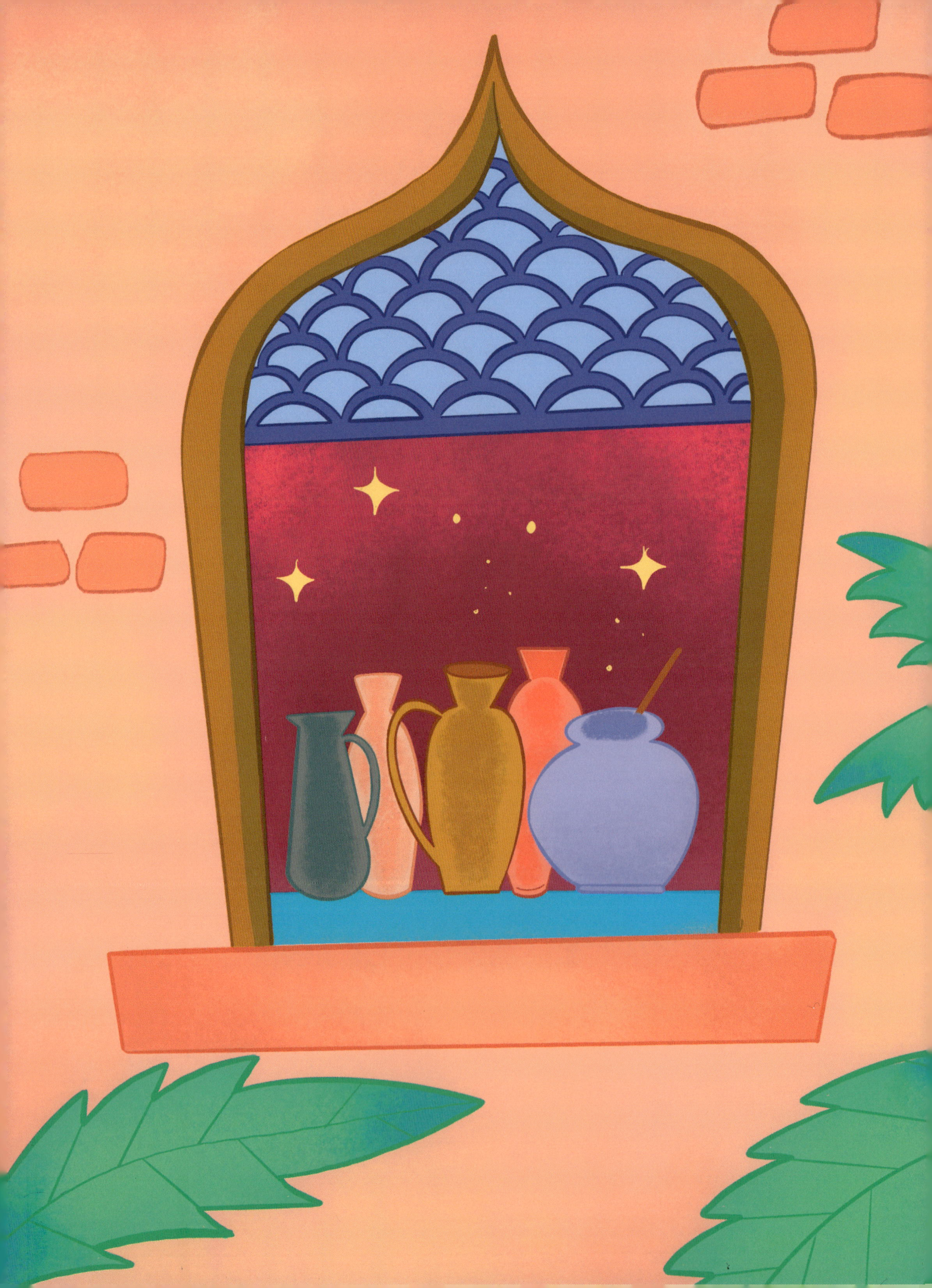

One day, t'was a Wednesday

The girls announced, randomly (or not), like all little ones do, "We know we can all have superpowers, and we know we have one too

So we've been thinking hard about it mama."

"We want to save lives like real-superheroes do!

We want to spread good and serve our community

A hero like Al-Shifa bint Abdullah we too want to be"

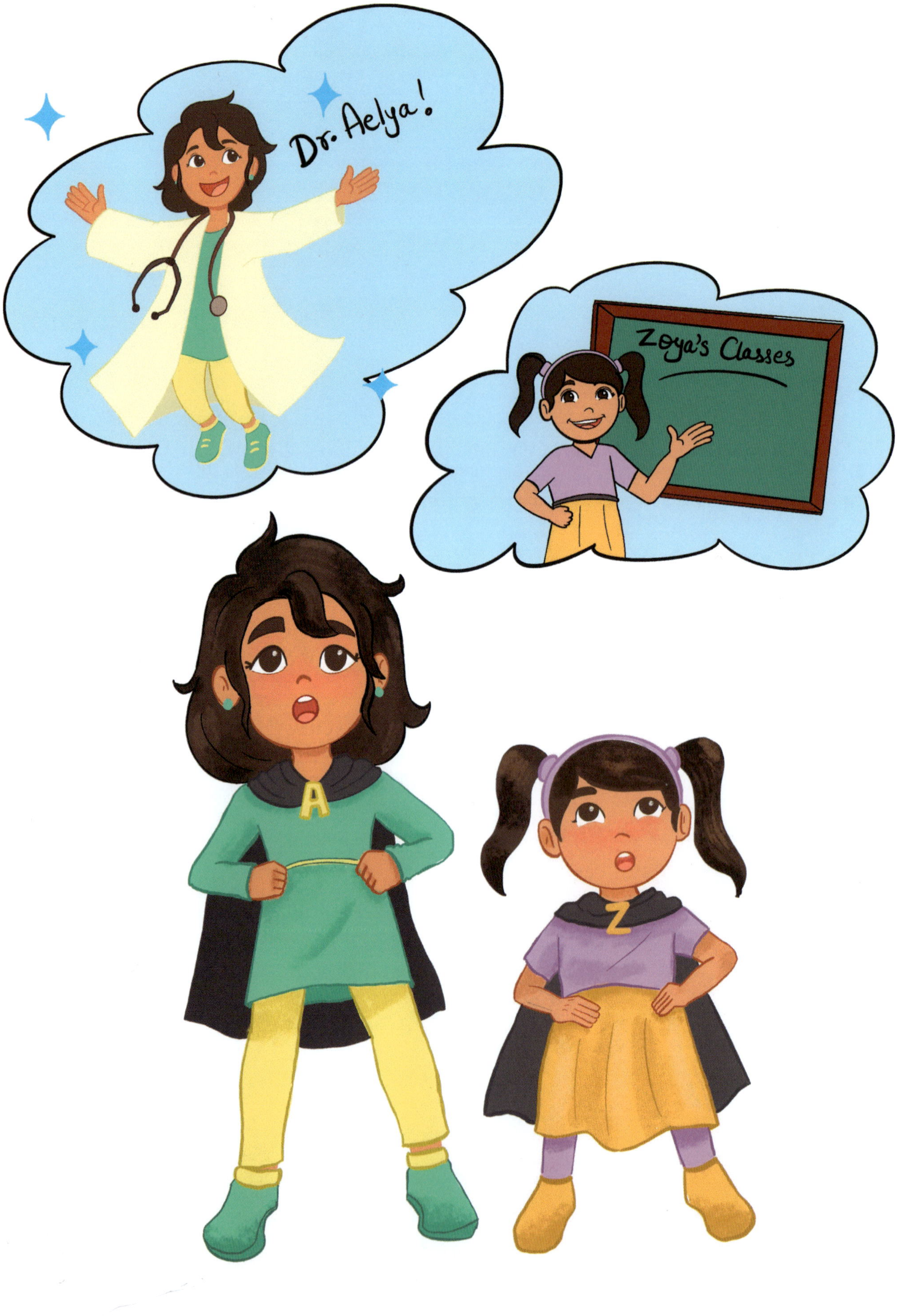
Dr. Aelya!
Zoya's Classes

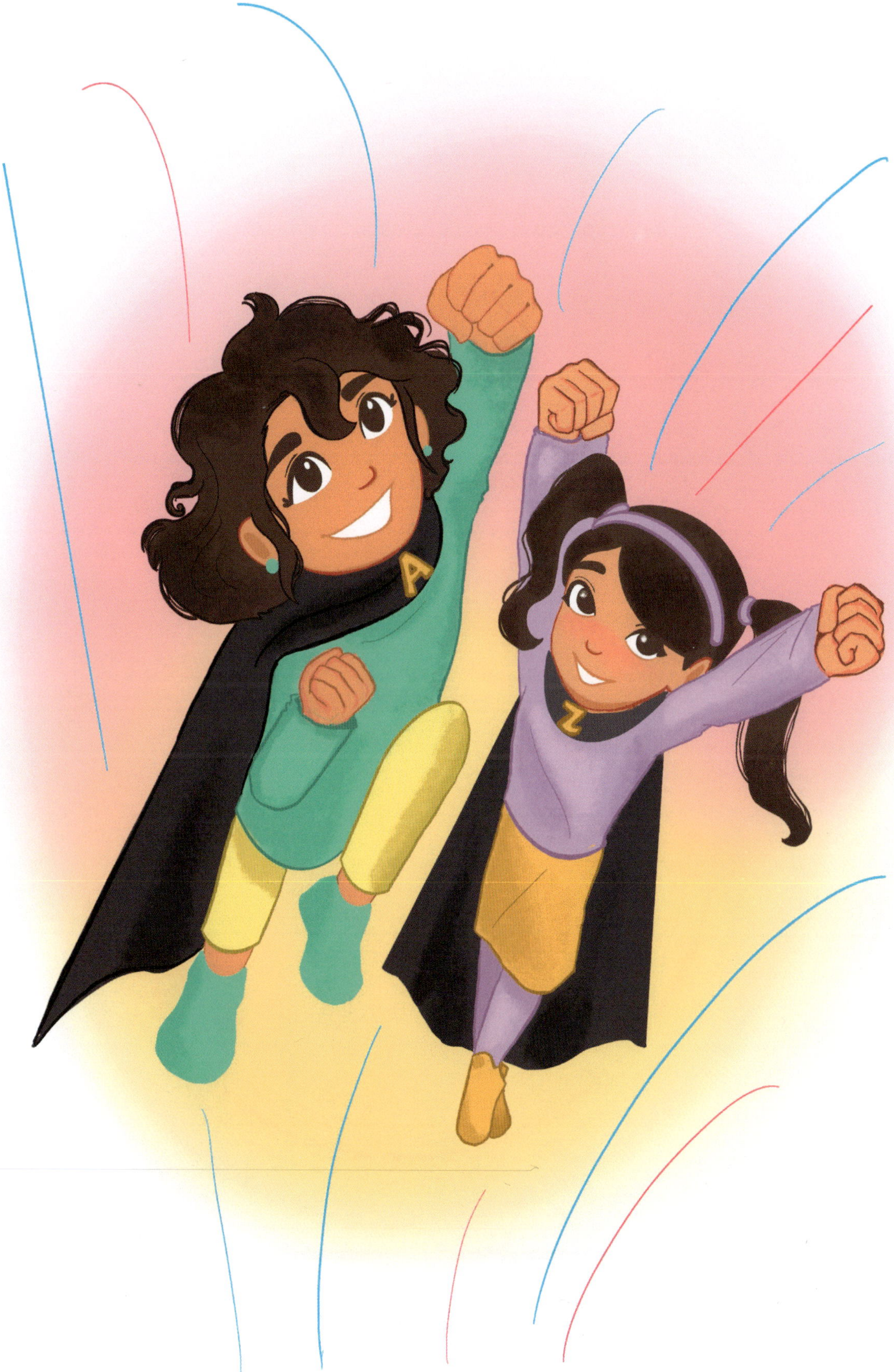

Superheroes are every where, even if they don't have gadgets and capes. The Muslim women in this series are testimony to the fact that Muslim women are brave, wise and strong and have changed history with the power of their work for as long as history itself.

Since 1400 years they have been curing the sick, building havens of learning, strengthening and steering communities, leading armies and empowering nations with the power of their spoken word, pen, will power and brain.

To find out more about the other books in this series, visit
www.amazingmuslimsuperheroes.com

MEET THE CREATORS!

Fiza Asar - The Author

Fiza is a Masters from SOAS (London) in Media and Post-National Communication. Those are big words but what she remembers best from her times in school and college, are the stories she read about change-makers and thinkers who believe in the power of their pen and brains! She currently lives in Karachi, Pakistan and now her three kids love reading books about amazing girls and boys (and animals) from around the world who spread love through their intelligence and courage. She also spends her time thinking about ways she can inspire her three kids into becoming real superheroes. Or is it the other way round?

Tehreem Iqbal - The Illustrator

Tehreem is an illustrator by profession who has had the passion for creativity since childhood. She brings out her imagination through her canvas and considers art her 'Superpower.' Her way of story-telling is through illustrations.

Amazing Muslim SuperHERoes

HISTORICAL NOTE FOR THE GROWN-UPS!

Layla bint Abdallah (popularly knows as al-Shifa because of her healing powers) was amongst the first healers in Islam. She was the daughter of Abdullah bin Shams and Fatima bint Wahab and grew up in Mecca, Arabia. Layla could not only read and write, but she was also a thinker who had a passion for the sciences of healing. It is believed that she discovered the remedy to ant bites and demonstrated it for the Prophet Muhammad (pbuh) who is said to have been so impressed, that he advised her to teach the method to his wife.

This little incident in itself shows how women have always been respected and regarded for their knowledge and personality and the Holy Prophet (PBUH), encouraged this in the women of his family and community and for women in general. It shows the importance Islam lays on knowledge and science, and how significant it was for Muhammad (PBUH) to encourage Muslims to take care of their health and wellbeing.

AND THEN MAMA DESCRIBES HOW ANT STINGS CAN BE CURED. THEY IMPERSONATE IT!

If you're sure you've been stung by an ant or a bee, here are some natural remedies Aelya and Zoya's mama swears by:

1. Apply a small amount of lemon juice and help reduce the discomfort

2. Honey can reduce redness, swelling and itching!

3. A thin slice of cucumber applied on the ant bite can really calm the itch down

4. White toothpastes can work wonders too. And if you don't have those, good old natural toothpaste can be made with baking soda mixed in some water - apply this not on your teeth, but the itch!

5. Simply rub olive oil on the ant bite and see it go!

Historians conclude
Caliph Umar*, told all tradesmen, salespersons, and shopkeepers, there better be no scam
Listen to "Market Controller" Al-Shifa - her laws of fair trade are according to Islam
In the days when men didn't read or write, and women even less so
Here was a woman the master of education, health and finance - a genius it is true!

Being a doctor and the mother of 2 daughters myself, I have always craved stories of women heroes, and ideals for the future generations to come. This visual true story of Al - Shifa Bin Abdullah written by Fiza Asar gives us hope and tells us what true Islamic female heroes are like and has the power to inspire the upcoming girls in a very interesting yet simple language that if they believe in themselves, they can reach the highest levels of success. It also teaches that Islam is a religion that truly empowers women which is so much needed in today's time and hour for our part of the world"

Dr. Iffat Zafar Aga
Cofounder & COO Sehat Kahani

OH NO! Our petite but brave Zoya got a bee sting... mama is using weird medicine to heal it, which got us intrigued to learn more about ancient medicine remedies. Read this book to join us in our adventure to learn about olden times medicine and an extraordinary woman who was a natural healer in this extremely captivating story from 1400 years ago.

Madiha Rehman
Director Programs,
AzCorp Entertaiment Private Limited

Printed in Great Britain
by Amazon